Benjamin Franklin

by Wil Mara

Content Consultant
Nanci R. Vargus, Ed.D.
Professor Emeritus, University of Indianapolis

Reading Consultant
Jeanne Clidas, Ph.D.
Reading Specialist

Children's Press®
An Imprint of Scholastic Inc.
New York Toronto London Auckland Sydney
Mexico City New Delhi Hong Kong
Danbury, Connecticut

Library of Congress Cataloging-in-Publication Data
Mara, Wil.
 Benjamin Franklin/by Wil Mara; poem by Jodie Shepherd. — [New edition].
    pages cm. — (Rookie biographies)
 Includes bibliographical references and index.
 ISBN 978-0-531-20558-7 (library binding: alk. paper) — ISBN 978-0-531-21201-1 (pbk.: alk. paper)
 1. Franklin, Benjamin, 1706-1790—Juvenile literature. 2. Statesmen—United States—
Biography—Juvenile literature. 3. Scientists—United States—Biography—Juvenile
literature. 4. Inventors—United States—Biography—Juvenile literature. 5. Printers—
United States—Biography—Juvenile literature. I. Shepherd, Jodie. II. Title.

 E302.6.F8M28 2014
  973.3092—dc23 [B]   2014015037

Produced by Spooky Cheetah Press
Poem by Jodie Shepherd
Design by Keith Plechaty

Printed in China 62

SCHOLASTIC, CHILDREN'S PRESS, ROOKIE BIOGRAPHIES®, and associated logos
are trademarks and/or registered trademarks of Scholastic Inc.

1 2 3 4 5 6 7 8 9 10 R 24 23 22 21 20 19 18 17 16 15

Photographs © 2015: Alamy Images: cover (Archive Images), 11 (Everett Collection
Historical), 28 (JJM Stock Photography), 27 (North Wind Picture Archives), 24 (Old
Paper Studios); Getty Images/Prism/UIG: 3 top right, 30 top right; Science Source/
Photo Researchers, Inc.: 4, 30 top left; Superstock, Inc.: 31 bottom (Exactostock),
16 (National Portrait Gallery), 23; The Granger Collection: 12, 15 inset, 20; The
Image Works: 19 (akg-images), 8, 31 center bottom (Newagen Archive), 15 (North
Wind Picture Archives), 3 bottom, 31 top (SSPL/Science Museum); Thinkstock/
UmbertoPantalone: 3 top left.

Table of Contents

4

Meet Benjamin Franklin

Benjamin Franklin is one of the most important figures in American history. He is one of America's "Founding Fathers."

Franklin was born in Boston, Massachusetts, on January 17, 1706. He loved to read and learn new things. Young Ben had to leave school when he was 10 so he could get a job. He began working with his brother, who was a **printer**. But Franklin kept reading all the time.

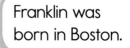
Franklin was born in Boston.

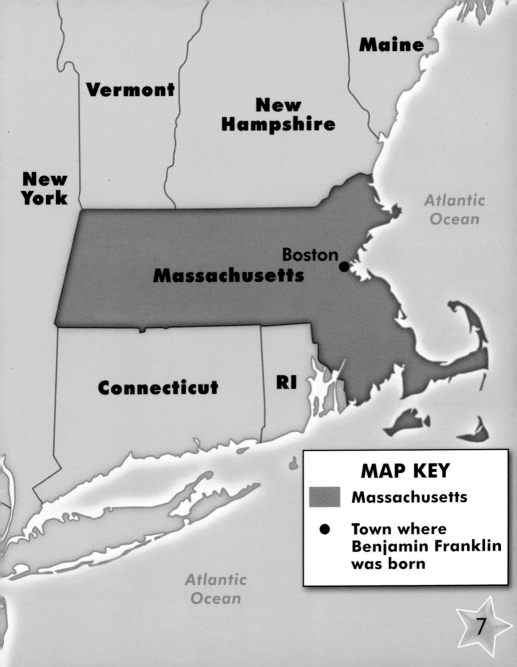

Maine

Vermont

New
Hampshire

New
York

Atlantic
Ocean

Boston •

Massachusetts

Connecticut

RI

Atlantic
Ocean

MAP KEY

Massachusetts

● Town where
Benjamin Franklin
was born

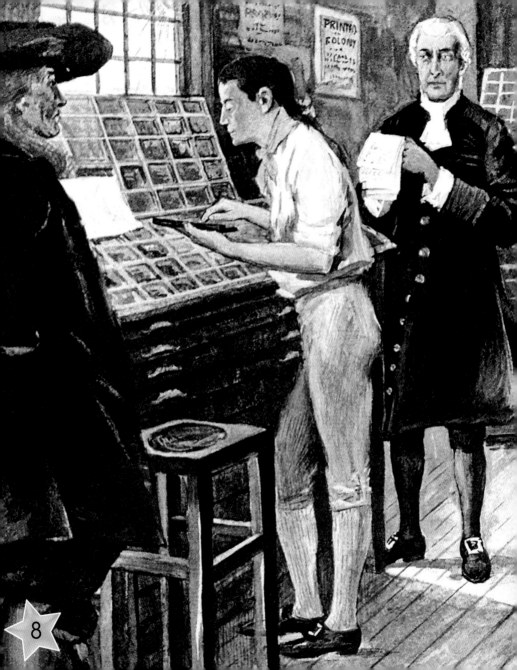

A Successful Young Man

When he was 17, Franklin moved to Philadelphia, Pennsylvania. He quickly found work as a printer. During this time, he met Deborah Read.

Franklin and Deborah had two children together. Their son, Francis, was born in October 1732. He lived only four years. Their daughter, Sarah, was born in September 1744.

FAST FACT!

Once a year, Franklin published a book called *Poor Richard's Almanack*. It became very popular. Although Franklin wrote it under a different name, most of his readers knew he was the author!

A Brilliant Mind

By the 1730s, Franklin had become famous for his writings. Many of his other projects were meant to help people. He started a fire department and created a library in his hometown.

Franklin founded the Library Company of Philadelphia.

Franklin was also a talented inventor. In 1742, he created a type of stove that kept houses warmer than ever before. One of his most famous inventions came in his later life. His **bifocal** eyeglasses had lenses that helped a person see both up close and far away.

FAST FACT!

Franklin did not invent electricity, but he did discover many new facts about it.

lenses for seeing far away

bifocals

lenses for seeing close up

War!

Pennsylvania was one of 13 British **colonies**. Many people living in the colonies were becoming angry at their British rulers. They felt King George was treating them unfairly. In 1775, the Americans went to war against Great Britain.

King George was the ruler of Great Britain from 1760 to 1820.

In 1776, Franklin helped write the Declaration of Independence. It stated that the colonists were no longer under Great Britain's rule.

Franklin works on the Declaration of Independence with Thomas Jefferson and others.

Benjamin Franklin

Thomas Jefferson

20

In December 1776, Franklin went to France to ask for help with the war. The French government sent thousands of soldiers to America. After six years of fighting, the British finally surrendered.

In 1783, Franklin signed the Treaty of Paris in France. The war was officially over.

Franklin meets the King and Queen of France.

American Hero

When Franklin returned to America in 1785, he was very old. He chose to work on projects that were important to him. Franklin had owned some slaves in the past. Now he gave them their freedom. He said **slavery** in the United States should be stopped.

23

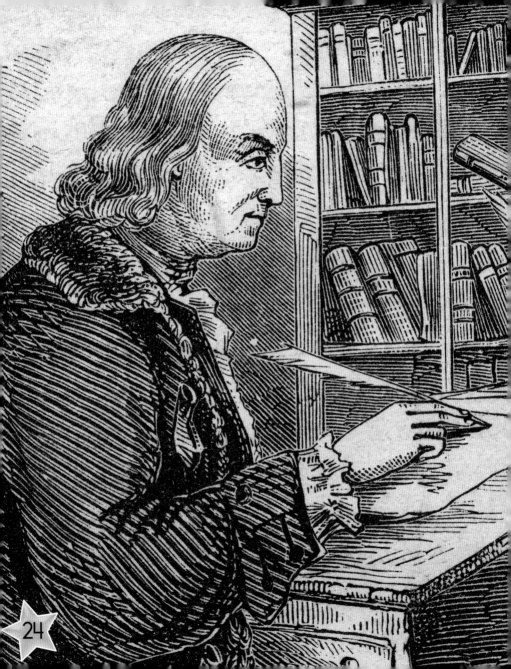

During this time, Franklin stayed mostly at home. He enjoyed spending time with his daughter, Sarah, and his grandchildren. Franklin also wrote the story of his life. It is called *The Autobiography of Benjamin Franklin.*

In 1787, leaders from the 13 states met to decide how their new country should be run. Franklin was one of the people who represented Pennsylvania. Together the leaders created the United States Constitution.

Franklin meets with Alexander Hamilton and other American leaders to create the U.S. Constitution.

Alexander Hamilton

27

Timeline of Benjamin Franklin's Life

1729
begins publishing *The Pennsylvania Gazette*

1775
Revolutionary War begins

1706
born on January 17

1733
begins publishing *Poor Richard's Almanack*

Franklin died in his Philadelphia home on April 17, 1790. He was 84 years old. Ben Franklin was one of those rare people who truly changed the world. It is hard to imagine what America would have become without him.

1783
helps write the Treaty of Paris, ending the war

1790
dies on April 17

1776
signs the Declaration of Independence

1787
signs the United States Constitution

29

A Poem About Benjamin Franklin

Born in Boston, taught a trade at ten,

Good at so many things was Ben:

scientist, publisher, inventor, and writer,

and heroic American freedom fighter.

You Can Be a Leader

- Do not be afraid to think differently. That is when the best ideas will come.

- Be willing to stand up for what you believe is right.

- Work hard every day. Ben believed that the only way to success was to be *productive*.